# DAMON HILL

*World Champion*

# DAMON HILL

## World Champion

---

### The Triumphant Story of a
### British Sporting Hero

---

David Tremayne

First published in Great Britain in 1996 by
Parragon Book Service Ltd
Unit 13–17
Avonbridge Trading Estate
Atlantic Road
Avonmouth
Bristol BS11 9QD

ISBN: 0-7525-2013-X


Produced by Haldane Mason, London

*Art Director:* Ron Samuels
*Editor:* Tessa Rose
*Design:* Digital Artworks Partnership Ltd
*Picture Research:* Charles Dixon-Spain


Printed in Italy

## *PICTURE CREDITS*

**LAT Photographic:** 2, 6 (*all*), 9, 10, 11, 12, 13, 14, 15, 16, 17, 18, 19, 20 (*all*), 23, 29, 30 (*top & bottom right*), 33, 35, 40 (*top & bottom left*), 43 (*photographer*: Peter J. Fox), 45, 47, 48, 50 (*both*), 51, 52 (*top & bottom left*), 60, 61, 64, 66 (*all*), 69, 72, 74, 77, 79; **Behram Kapadia:** 25, 30 (*bottom left*), 34, 36, 37, 38, 39, 40 (*bottom right*), 44, 46, 52 (*bottom right*), 59, 76; **Sutton Motorsport:** 24, 26, 28, 55, 56, 58, 63, 65, 70–71, 78.


Every effort has been made to trace the copyright holders and we apologize in advance for any unintentional omissions. We would be pleased to insert the appropriate acknowledgement in any subsequent edition of this publication.

# CONTENTS

# CHAPTER 1

*Victories in Australia, Brazil and Argentina got Damon Hill off to the perfect start in his quest for the World Championship. Even when he stumbled in the Nurburgring, he quickly regained his momentum with a fourth triumph in San Marino. Then came costly retirements, in Monaco and Spain, before wins five and six in Canada and France. But the British GP proved a turning point, for it marked the first of his really poor starts, a retirement, and the emergence of Jacques Villeneuve's remarkable challenge. Behind the scenes, it also marked Frank Williams' decision to extend the option he had signed with Heinz-Harald Frentzen.*

*Hill won for the seventh time, in Germany, but thereafter Villeneuve had the upper hand. In September came a mistake at Monza, and defeat in Estoril which set up the showdown in Japan. By then, of course, Hill knew that whatever he did Williams did not want him for 1997, for the axe had fallen after the Belgian GP when Williams signed Frentzen. As he headed for Suzuka, seeking the last point he needed to clinch the crown, he already had a new contract to race for the TWR Arrows team. An era was about to come to an end, but still there was the mountain to climb.*

# A BITTERSWEET TRIUMPH

The sigh of relief that Damon Hill expelled at the end of the Japanese Grand Prix echoed around the globe, mingling with the strain of the National Anthem as Britain crowned her eighth World Champion since the series was inaugurated in 1950.

What had started as the year in which his destiny seemed pre-ordained, had degenerated into a cliffhanger tainted by the bitterness of his mid-season rejection by the team for whom his efforts over the past six years had reaped 20 race wins, 20 pole positions, 19 fastest laps and the majority of the points towards three Constructors' World Championships.

Hill was too dignified in public ever to let slip just how damaging a psychological blow Frank Williams struck him when, after the Belgian Grand Prix at Spa-Francorchamps in August, he brought negotiations over a 1997 contract to an end and instead signed the German driver Heinz-Harald Frentzen to partner Jacques Villeneuve. But the revelation coincided with a decline in Hill's overall level of competitiveness that might simply have been a coincidence and a product of the Canadian's growing confidence, or could equally have been induced by the deep feelings of injustice that Hill was left to harbour. It seemed that he was good enough to win the World Championship in 1996, but not good enough to keep for the long-term. For any competitive athlete, that must have been a devastating blow.

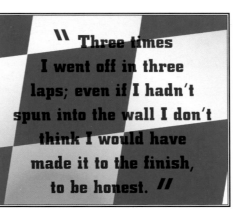

" Three times I went off in three laps; even if I hadn't spun into the wall I don't think I would have made it to the finish, to be honest. "

Hill's 1996 World Championship campaign could not have got off to a better start, with victories in Melbourne, Interlagos and Buenos Aires. At that stage his new partnership with Jacques Villeneuve appeared to be going well, and Michael Schumacher's struggle with his new Ferrari, allied to Benetton's loss of pace as it adjusted to life without the World Champion, buoyed him with hope. Nevertheless, he refused to become complacent, saying: 'Threats are coming from a number of directions. We have a wide base of competition. You can't rule out either of the Benettons, and, of course, you can't rule out Michael and Ferrari. There may be others.'

**Hill congratulates Villeneuve on his superb debut in Melbourne, where the young Canadian led until making a mistake that damaged an oil line and obliged him to surrender the initiative. Later the relationship would become more strained as they fought down to the wire at Suzuka.**

The European Grand Prix at the Nurburgring, which kicked off the European season in April, interrupted the flow, when Villeneuve won and Hill was fortunate to salvage fourth place after a series of adventures, but Hill dominated again in Imola and was crushing everybody at Monaco – including Schumacher, who crashed on the first lap trying to keep up – until a rare Renault engine failure robbed him of a fifth win. Schumacher made comprehensive

amends in Spain with a brilliant performance on a wet track from which Hill departed with an embarrassing spin on the pit straight. Hill was back on form to vanquish Villeneuve on the latter's home ground in Montreal.

As usual, he did not try to shift blame for his mistakes in Spain, though others have attempted to offer them for him. 'It was lack of changes to the car that made it so difficult to drive,' he said. 'We were

**Wife, friend and helpmate, Georgie Hill proves that behind every good man there is a good woman. In the dark hours of 1994, and again in 1996, Damon drew strongly on her unwavering support.**

reluctant – I was reluctant – to change the car because it was in very similar specification to the morning. It was fantastic then, but it rained a bit more. On the grid I said it was a lot wetter than it was that morning, but I didn't really press the point hard enough. Obviously the car felt good in the wet in the morning and I was confident of my abilities in the wet, but it caught us out quite a lot, really. I was kicking myself a lot for that race, because I felt it was as much my fault as anybody else's.

'I simply couldn't attack at all with the car. It wasn't so much that it was aquaplaning; it had too much oversteer. It was just a nightmare! Locking up the rear under braking. Three times I went off in three

laps; even if I hadn't spun into the wall I don't think I would have made it to the finish, to be honest. It would have spun, even driving slowly. In conditions like that you can't drive slowly, you've got to attack, and I couldn't attack because the car was just too nervous.'

Nor did he dwell on Monaco. 'I've forgotten about Monaco now,' he said soon afterwards. 'It didn't take me long to get over it. I'm not looking back at all. The warning light came on, then everything stopped about a lap later. It was fairly quick.'

On the eve of the Canadian GP he maintained a perspective. 'Let's put it this way: I've still got a car capable of winning Grands Prix. Yes, others now may also have them but that's okay because I've won four races already so I have those in the bank. If I equal the number of wins of any other driver between now and the end of the season, then I still have the advantage I have got now. So potentially it's still looking very good for the championship.'

Since 1995 he had developed into a far more resilient character, and if the recent setbacks troubled him he had a good way of hiding it. 'It seems to be more a problem in the minds of everyone else. It's a point that's being asked because it's a change in the storyline, but the truth of the matter is that nothing much has changed. I still have the chance to win races and I still have the chance to win the championship.'

At the halfway point he was 21 points clear of Villeneuve, and another Williams one-two in France boosted the gap to 25. Such was Hill's superiority that observers already regarded the championship as won.

Bernie Ecclestone was asked his opinion of the man he had not rated in 1995, and replied: 'I thought Jacques would blow the 1995 Damon away, but this year Damon has raised his performance incredibly. He's very determined, and very focused. I think he's doing a very good job and making the best of his ability.'

But at the British GP things began to unravel. From pole position Hill made a poor start, and after running fourth he retired when a front wheel worked loose. Villeneuve won. Advantage 15 points.

He bounced back with a lucky win in Germany, when Gerhard Berger's engine blew up within

sight of the Hockenheim flag, and Villeneuve was only third. Advantage 21 points again.

Before Hockenheim, however, the British weekly magazine *Autosport* had suggested that Frentzen had already been signed to replace Hill for 1997. It transpired that at that stage the deal had not actually been done, but the net effect was unsettling, and it showed in Hill's driving. At the same time, his tardy starts were becoming a cause for deep concern. It was no good qualifying on pole, only to surrender the advantage on getaway. Hill preferred the traditional three-pedal control – throttle, brake, clutch – whereas

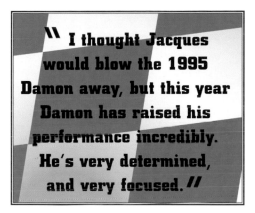

" I thought Jacques would blow the 1995 Damon away, but this year Damon has raised his performance incredibly. He's very determined, and very focused. "

**Hill chases hard after Gerhard Berger's Benetton at Hockenheim, where the Austrian seemed set to win the German GP until his engine broke in the closing laps. For Hill the four extra points would be vital.**

**Facing the press: At Monza Hill withstood media assault as they tried to make sense of why Frank Williams had taken the decision to drop Hill in favour of Heinz-Harold Frentzen.**

Villeneuve liked the two-pedal system – throttle, brake – and hand operated clutch.

'With a hand clutch and only two pedals, you have the possibility of putting your right foot on the throttle and the left hard on the brake while simultaneously letting the clutch out until you feel the car straining against the brakes as the clutch bites,' explained Patrick Head, Williams' technical director. 'And then taking your foot off the brakes when the lights change. You have found the bite point, at which the clutch starts gripping. You have found that in advance of the start, so all you have got to do is take your foot straight off the brake pedal and boompf! You're going.

'The problem for Damon is that he's got three pedals and only two feet. And if he's got one foot on the accelerator and one foot on the clutch, he hasn't got one for the brake. So when the lights change he's got to take his foot back on the clutch and find just the right point at which it is gripping to produce drive, but not get so much grip at low speed that it bogs the engine down. He's got to find that point, whereas Jacques has already found that point before the off.'

It happened again in Hungary. Losing out at the start Hill had to try to haul Villeneuve in. They finished seconds apart. Advantage 17 points.

**First Silverstone, then Hockenheim, and then Hungary. Each time poor starts cost Hill enormously. Here at Hungaroring pole-winner Schumacher is already leading from Villeneuve and Alesi, both of whom started behind Hill on the grid.**

**Every picture tells a story, and here at Monza (far right) it was one of nightmare as Hill threw away a commanding lead after impressing everyone with his aggressive push towards first place.**

And then came Spa. Robbed of his chance of pole by rain, Hill spun briefly in the race morning warm-up, but he and Renault only belatedly realized he had counter-rotated his car's engine in the incident. By the time they did it was too late to change it, and Hill went to the line in the spare Williams. Again he made a bad start, and his race was deeply disappointing. Schumacher won after Villeneuve misheard a radio instruction to make his refuelling stop. That meant he would have to stop a lap later, when Hill was due in. There would not be room for both at once. Damon was on the pit entry when he was told to stay out, and lost a lot of time rejoining the track. Worse still, he made a meal of trying to overtake Martin Brundle in the Jordan-Peugeot, a combination that should have given the Williams-Renault very little trouble. Frank Williams took note.

On a day of disaster, Villeneuve was second, Hill only fifth. Advantage 13 points. And by the following Wednesday Frank had decided that he would opt for Frentzen, with his reputation as the man who was as quick as Schumacher in their karting days and their time as partners in the Mercedes-Benz sportscar team. Williams never made it clear whether he doubted Hill's ability to fight on even terms in 1997 if Schumacher had a fully competitive Ferrari, or whether he just got tired of dealing with Hill's manager, London-based solicitor Michael Breen. It didn't really matter, for the damage was done and the news was out.

At Monza Hill should have dominated the race after taking pole position, overtaking Alesi on the first lap, and then defending his position against counter-attack. But he spun on the sixth lap, in a terrible faux

**Shrugging off the drama of his sacking by Williams, Hill had responded aggressively by taking pole position in qualifying.**

pas that cost him the chance of clinching the title in style. The only thing that prevented Frank from saying 'I told you so' was that both Villeneuve and Frentzen made similar errors.

Hill could have clinched things at Estoril, but after he had led he lost time in traffic, just as Villeneuve was on a charge after passing Schumacher – of all people – round the outside of the last corner, which is named after Ayrton Senna. Villeneuve beat him fair and square that day, and Hill slowed later with a clutch problem, his advantage now down to

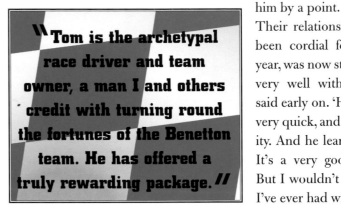

**"Tom is the archetypal race driver and team owner, a man I and others credit with turning round the fortunes of the Benetton team. He has offered a truly rewarding package. //**

nine points. If Villeneuve won in Suzuka and Hill failed to finish in the top six, the Canadian would beat him by a point.

Their relationship, which had been cordial for most of the year, was now strained. 'I get on very well with Jacques,' Hill said early on. 'He's very bright, very quick, and has a lot of ability. And he learns quickly, too. It's a very good relationship. But I wouldn't say it's the best I've ever had with a team-mate. He's just a team-mate. I don't have a chart in my head who is the best team-mate I've ever had; you can't do

**Look back in anguish. On the afternoon he could have clinched the World Championship, Hill walks away from his abandoned Williams after spinning out of the lead in the Italian GP. At that precise moment he must have wondered if he was also walking away from the title.**

that. People are simply different characters and it's style rather than anything else. I get on very well with Jacques. He gets on with his thing, he doesn't try to be too clever with me, and we work in the team together.' By Estoril, their body language hinted at a divide.

Before leaving for Suzuka, Hill had one vital move to make. When Ecclestone's efforts to slot him into Alesi's seat at Benetton failed after Monza, the F1 world had expected him to sign to drive alongside Schumacher's younger brother Ralf in the Jordan-Peugeot team, but Hill sprang a major surprise when he announced that he had agreed terms with Tom Walkinshaw to race for TWR Arrows.

'Tom is the archetypal race driver and team owner, a man I and others credit with turning round the fortunes of the Benetton team. He is the head of a successful international engineering team. He has offered me a truly rewarding package. It's a great challenge. Everything this man does and touches becomes a winner, and right now I am feeling very excited.'

The world was sceptical, suggesting that he had abandoned Jordan in favour of big money from TWR, but Hill had spent seven hours visiting its headquarters at Leafield, near Oxford. There he had viewed the wind tunnel, the state-of-the-art design department, the engine factory and the rest of the equipment that placed the team almost on a par with Williams. And he had been sufficiently impressed to agree with Walkinshaw's demand for a decision that

same day. His manager Michael Breen had spoken with Jordan on the Wednesday, they visited TWR the following day, and the deal was made public on Friday, 27 September.

'Nobody is under any illusion over the task ahead,' Hill said. 'Winning in Formula One is not easy. But I was left in no doubt that the package and facilities Tom has are the beginnings of what I believe will be a winning team.' If he felt embarrassed to switch from one of the most successful teams to one that had yet to win a single race in 287 tries, he hid it well.

'I have been pretty impressed with what I have seen of Damon's driving,' Walkinshaw said as he savoured his coup, 'and I have always wanted a topflight driver to lead this team.'

Only Suzuka, the last great mountain, remained to climb before he could begin his new life.

In the dying moments of qualifying in Suzuka, Hill pulled up to within half a second of Villeneuve as the Canadian took pole position, but the Englishman once again looked shaky. But at the start it was Villeneuve who made the error and Hill shot into a lead he would never lose.

Surviving a strong initial attack from Gerhard Berger, who nearly cost him everything with an ambitious lunge at the chicane, Damon became

**Meet the boss. Tom Walkinshaw's announcement that he had signed Hill from under the nose of Eddie Jordan took the F1 world by complete surprise.**

Britain's eighth World Champion on the 37th lap when Villeneuve, back in fourth place behind Schumacher and Mika Hakkinen, crashed when his car lost a rear wheel. Damon had driven a champion's race to take his 21st GP triumph, his eighth of the season, and to become the only World Champion's son in history to emulate his father's achievement.

'I felt great when I saw Jacques' start,' he admitted, 'but I also felt great at Monza, so I was just out there at front thinking: "This is all very well Hill; stay calm, and see it through to the finish. Just drive nice and easy." ' His overalls drenched in victory champagne, he added, 'It's a lot to take on board. It takes up a lot of your mental energy just doing a Grand Prix. When you've won the World Championship and the Grand Prix all in one race, it's a hell of a thing. Right now I feel like I'm on a rocket that's just taken off. It's just a wonderful release of pressure and sense of satisfaction.

'Fifteen laps from the end I got the message Jacques was out. But try and concentrate on the race when you realize you're World Champion! . . . It was a matter of just trying to put it out of my mind, if you can believe it, because the next job was to win the race and I really, really wanted to do that. This win was for the team, my leaving present. I'm really grateful to everyone there and everything they've done. But the championship is for me.

'It was absolutely perfect. I've worked for this and it's a tremendous relief to have won it and ended all the waiting, the training, the preparation, the testing and the sleepless nights! And all the anxiety for

Made it Ma, Top of the World! At Suzuka Hill finally had cause to celebrate, when at last he clinched the elusive World Championship. Now he could lay 1996 to rest, and look forward to the future. A good guy had won.

Georgie, who has really stood by me the whole way and been a tremendous strength and support.

'I think I am going to celebrate at least until Christmas, maybe a little beyond that. It's a great thing to have happened. You know, it could have gone the other way. I might have been standing here and Jacques could have been champion and I would have been feeling pretty sick, but I know Jacques is going to get another chance. He's young and he's quick and, to be honest, it had to be this year for me. I'm just really delighted.' As an indication of his quality as a man, Hill had paid for his most ardent fan, 17-year-old William Taylor, to attend the race. But typically Damon had kept this to himself.

Within Williams there was genuine pleasure. 'In many ways it's more appropriate for Damon to win, because he has worked hard for four years,' said Frank Williams. 'He's climbed the mountain, and he's now at the top. He deserves to be there.'

But it was Georgie Hill who summarized it best. 'I'm just so thrilled for him because he has worked so hard to get here. And all the people who thought he couldn't do it, that he wasn't good enough to do it, can now see that he has actually done it. And he's done it the hard way today. All the setbacks he's had, he's overcome and he's proved to himself to have more integrity and dignity in his little finger than most people have got in their whole body. And I'm just thrilled for him and really proud of him, because whatever you say, however many people everyone else thinks are helping him, it's only been Damon who has actually got in the car every time and done it.'

# CHAPTER 2

The legend of Graham Hill extended far beyond the realm of motorsport in the late Sixties and early Seventies and, even as his racing star began to wane, his popularity with the man in the street remained completely undimmed. The former champion was a personality as well as a celebrity, a distinctive swashbuckler with a wit sharper than a pirate's sword and charisma to charm television audiences as well as race fans.

Graham's death shattered his family, and his team and left a sport in mourning. His untimely end dramatically changed both the material and emotional circumstances of his family, but to their everlasting credit, his wife Bette, son Damon and daughters Brigitte and Samantha endured and survived with a fortitude and dignity that was as moving as it was laudable.

When the urge finally came upon Damon Hill to start racing himself, he did so initially on motorcycles at Brands Hatch, his father's old stamping ground. And when he switched to cars he discovered the hard way that there are no free lunches in a sport that had changed radically since the days when Jim Clark and Graham Hill raced wheel-to-wheel.

# FATHER AND SON

Many of today's television-nurtured race fans are only dimly aware that Damon Hill's father was a former World Champion. But diehard motorsport aficionados revere the memory of a man whose deep influence must inevitably be taken into account when his son's exploits are studied.

To a generation of motorsport enthusiasts across the globe in the Sixties, Graham Hill was Mr Motor Racing. With his dashing looks he was every inch a racing driver. There was the deep, forward-thrusting jaw, the erect bearing, the flowing hair and, latterly, the long sideburns; the clipped manner in which he spoke and, of course, the addition that topped it all – the military moustache that bristled an unmistakeable warning whenever the Hill temper was about to be vented. Long before fans of the Eighties and Nineties found themselves hyped along on a tide of Mansellmania, Graham Hill was the perfect ambassador for British motorsport. It was a role with which he was completely comfortable, for he loved the limelight. There

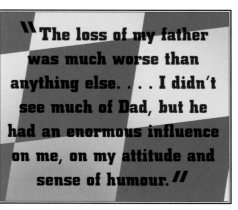

" The loss of my father was much worse than anything else. . . . I didn't see much of Dad, but he had an enormous influence on me, on my attitude and sense of humour. //

was genuine affection for him throughout the sport, and his wry but razor-sharp sense of humour was legendary. He loved his motor racing, and motor racing in turn loved him. Even the man in the street recognized just how much he had put back into the sport.

His widow Bette summed him up perfectly when she said: 'In the old days Graham would sit on a tyre signing autographs in the paddock. When he lost the 1960 British Grand Prix he walked back waving to the crowd and I thought to myself, "God, you are conceited!" But he wasn't, of course. He was just as good a loser as he was a winner.'

Graham Hill, the man who began as a mechanic and parlayed his ability with a spanner into regular drives in racing cars, evolved into a top-flight Grand Prix driver. He won 14 Grands Prix, driving for the BRM and Lotus teams. A record five of them were at Monaco where, in the mid-Sixties, it seemed that he, not Prince Rainier, owned the Principality. The World Championship twice surrendered to him, in 1962 and again in 1968, and he took a surprise victory in America's glittering Indianapolis 500 classic in 1966. Six years later he

This motor-racing lark is all a bit dull really, isn't it Dad? Eight year-old Damon Hill follows his own thoughts as Graham concentrates on practice for the Italian Grand Prix at Monza in 1968. Twenty-eight years later, Damon's expression – at the same track – would not have changed much, even if his circumstances had.

added the Le Mans 24 Hours to his tally of major victories. No other man has ever worn the remarkable Triple Crown, which is based upon the trilogy of the world's most famous races: Monaco, Indy and Le Mans.

This, then, was the man whose influence would shadow his son's career long after the dank, foggy night of 29 November 1975 when Hill flew back from Marseilles with most of the small F1 team he had formed two years earlier. The CAA Certificate of Airworthiness on his Piper Aztec had, unknown to him, been allowed to lapse, and the altimeter was incorrectly calibrated. He was advised to detour to Luton Airport further to the north, but the men's cars were all parked at Elstree's small aerodrome, just to the north of London. Hill took the special route in taught to him by Lotus chief Colin Chapman, but because of the incorrect calibration of the altimeter Hill was lower than he thought and the plane came down in trees on the Arkley Golf Course. Everyone

**Motorcycles, not cars, were Hill's first love. Having missed out the karting stage that many feel is vital for subsequent motor-racing success, Damon cut his teeth racing a variety of machines at Brands Hatch.**

aboard – Hill, his massively talented protégé Tony Brise, designer Andy Smallman, team manager Ray Brimble and mechanics Terry Richards and Tony Alcock – perished.

Seventeen years after the tragedy, Damon Hill prepared to take the same Oxford blue helmet and its famous eight vertical white flashes representing the oar blades of the London Rowing Club into Formula One battle again. Graham always joked that he liked sports that let him sit down but Damon carried the colours simply because they were his father's. It was a nice emotional touch, but he is careful to keep his antecedents and his own achievements in perspective.

In England, being the scion of a famous family can be a double-edged sword. For a young racer it can open doors, but it can also saddle him with a lot of emotional baggage and the preconceptions of others. In America, sons attempting to emulate the deeds of famous fathers are actively encouraged, as Al Unser Jnr and Michael Andretti will testify. But in Europe you have to go back to Alberto Ascari before you find a son whose own performances earned him what some purists perceive as the right to be compared with an illustrious parent, or look forward to Hill's Williams team-mate Jacques Villeneuve, son of the late Ferrari legend Gilles.

For Hill the tragedy had many components, for at 15 he had only just been getting to know a father who was frequently absent, who probably spent more time with Brise, and whose life was at times tangled and complicated. In the immediate aftermath his mother Bette sent him abroad to stay in California with Dan Gurney, the great American racer who was Graham's team-mate in 1960, and with Phil Hill, the 1961 World Champion who was no relation but a good friend. Both of them were disturbed by the teenager's continuous withdrawn manner, but one day his frustration and grief simply exploded in rantings of pure anger.

The desperate readjustments that Graham Hill's family had to make were financial as well as emotional, for the shortcomings on his aeroplane paperwork invalidated the insurance. The families of the other victims made heavy claims on his estate.

Even today, Damon chooses his words carefully when he talks about his background.

'It's wrong to say having a famous dad was difficult. Of course there were the advantages of fame and wealth – a trials bike, good education, nice holidays. But from the first moment at primary school you'd be singled out; people would smile at you and make references. I was six when Dad won Indy, eight when he took his second World Championship. I didn't give a jot then, but people around you respond. It could be embarrassing in front of friends, when you wanted to be the same as them, not different. But it wasn't difficult; I didn't know anything different.

'The loss of my father was much worse than anything else. You can always replace things, but you can't reverse the death of your father. I didn't feel anything about what happened for years, although some of the aftermath made me very angry at times. Sometimes now I keep feeling it would be nice to have had a father around, so we could share things together. I didn't see much of Dad, but he had an enormous influence on me, on my attitude and sense of humour.'

He once said: 'I don't really mind being seen as Graham Hill's son, but it does get tedious when people keep wanting to do the old story "What does your mother think about you wanting to follow your father's footsteps?" '

His father bought him a trials bike, saying he was a natural rider, and it was bikes that initially interested him. After seeing Barry Sheene and Kenny Roberts in the Transatlantic races at Brands Hatch in 1976, he began thinking of racing himself, but he never really discovered whether Graham would have approved. He was reasonably successful on bikes at the Kentish circuit where, in 1983, the enterprising and publicity-conscious managing director John Webb organized an opportunity for him to race a car. This was an Argo JM16 Formula Ford 2000, in the BBC Television *Grandstand* series. One leading F3 team manager witnessed his early races, and later said of them: 'I felt sorry for the kid. He just didn't seem to have a clue what he was doing.' That would change.

**Graham Hill and Jim Clark (right) were the kings of the track in their day, and latterly team-mates at Lotus. Neither ever let their rivalry get in the way of their friendship.**

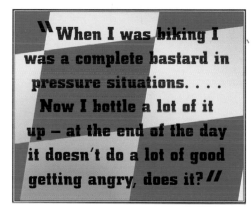

"When I was biking I was a complete bastard in pressure situations. . . . Now I bottle a lot of it up – at the end of the day it doesn't do a lot of good getting angry, does it?"

Hill admitted: 'Cars were a total culture shock!' But he persisted, graduating to Formula Three and then to Formula 3000, one step below Formula One. Along the way he borrowed £100,000 from a source he still refuses to identify. He had read one of the books written by former world champion Niki Lauda, and his mind was set. 'I figured if I was really convinced I could do it I'd take a gamble and let things sort themselves out. I borrowed a huge sum on the understanding that it would be paid back.' Just as Lauda had done.

History remembers Graham Hill as a relentless trier who made up what he might have lacked in sheer talent with persistence and commitment. He never gave up. He was an opportunist who made every situation work for him, and Damon would do the same. The money he borrowed financed a season of F3 in 1986, and the following year he was paid to drive for another team, which was sponsored by Cellnet, the mobile telephone network. He stayed with them for two years, and he won races, but the age-old sponsorship problems that British drivers usually face arose as he tried to graduate to F3000. Damon adopted a simple policy: drive whatever was available, no matter how bad it was. One of the poor cars he tried was called a Footwork, a Japanese car built by the team that would later sponsor the Arrows F1 team. It was crude and ineffective, but to Hill it was a godsend.

'People asked me "Why drive such a heap of junk?" ' he said. 'But if you can't drive anything else, you've got to drive something, haven't you? If you stand still you're not going anywhere. I had no sponsorship. So I decided whatever opportunity I get of driving a car, I'm going to have to make bloody good use of it because it might be the last chance.'

Damon Hill made his own luck. He'd been unable to raise the finance to go F3000, but travelled in hope to the first race at Silverstone. There he met entrant Colin Bennett, who offered him a few national F3000 races. Having no other offers, Hill accepted – and his performances led to a drive at Le Mans for Richard Lloyd's Porsche team. He kept going, and he always gave of his best.

'I was picking drives,' he recalled, 'not through bringing any money but because people thought I was capable and needed somebody to put in the car.'

His name stayed in the frame, and that helped when the Footwork opportunity arose. His race performances and technical feedback in that uncompetitive car led directly to the chance to race as a paid driver for the Middlebridge Lola team in 1990. That, finally, would be the turning point. That year, and 1991, saw him driving a car capable of winning races. He led frequently, and though the car usually broke, he was able to prove himself.

This was all crucial. In Formula One Williams was looking for a new test driver after Hill's F3 rival, Mark Blundell, had moved on to race for the Brabham F1 team. Frank Williams liked Hill's ability to lead races. In December 1991 Williams finally signed him, and he did so because Hill was quick and would fit in. He didn't sign him because he was Graham Hill's

**Opposite: Ricoh, the sponsor that left Hill in the lurch in 1986, made something of a comeback for the 1987 season, when Hill joined the Intersport Racing F3 team to drive professionally in the colours of Cellnet, the mobile communications network.**

boy, for there is no room for such sentiment in F1. He had made his own luck by going out to find it, instead of sitting at home complaining and waiting for miracles.

It was said of Graham Hill that he lacked Jim Clark's natural flair, that he really had to work at everything he did. The same has been said of Nigel Mansell in comparison with Ayrton Senna and, to an extent, about Hill compared to Michael Schumacher. Yet all three 'lesser' talents have nevertheless enjoyed high levels of success. Now, by happy irony, one of racing's wheels had come full circle. If Damon Hill had much in common with Mansell, and Mansell was the last man successfully to parlay test driving duties into a regular drive in his Lotus days, there was something wholly apposite that Hill, the latest graduate to follow such a route, should replace him at Williams.

'The parallel is very similar to Nigel getting the drive at Lotus,' Hill agreed. 'Colin Chapman thought the bloke was worth giving a chance and signed the contract. Yes, I think that's quite a close comparison.'

Like Mansell's, Hill's results weren't great before he got to F1. 'My CV is pretty miserable, really, by comparison to a lot of these guys, who win Vauxhall Lotus, Formula Three, Formula 3000,' he admitted. If I'd had the backing earlier on I think I might have had one of those titles, but then I'm not complaining

about anything.' He very rarely did. Despite the unhappy circumstances of his father's death, and the family's sudden need to adapt to a paler set of colours – or perhaps because of that – Damon Hill has never come across as a bitter or jaded man, even in the darkest moments when his career seemed to have stalled.

From an early stage he established a solid working relationship with Patrick Head, and was quick to acknowledge the help that the Williams technical director gave him in settling in. 'While he made it clear that I needed to do the job in the car, in the early days he was always very encouraging and gave me room, if you like, to make the odd mistake and to learn the ropes. When I first started in the test he said, "Just build up very gently. We're not expecting you to go

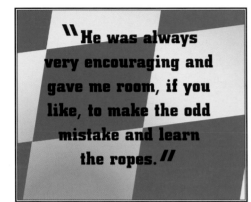

"**He was always very encouraging and gave me room, if you like, to make the odd mistake and learn the ropes.**"

**Formula Three was good to Hill in 1987. Here he celebrates success with his most indefatigable supporters, girlfriend Georgie (whom he subsequently married) and mother Bette.**

and break the lap record. We just want to get the work done." He made it easy for me to start with.'

Prior to races Graham Hill could be withdrawn, a formidable figure, wound up tight with concentration. Then, the national hero became Mr Hyde, dangerously unapproachable. Damon is easier-going, but admits he's a very self-analytical character. 'When I was biking I was a complete bastard in pressure situations. I would scream and shout at people. Now I bottle a lot of it up – at the end of the day it doesn't do a lot of good getting angry, does it?'

Hill draws heavily on his family for moral and practical support. His mother Bette and sisters Brigitte and Samantha are great pillars of strength and encouragement, and his great helpmate is his wife Georgie. Damon and Georgie have three children, sons Oliver and Joshua, and daughter Tabitha. Oliver was born with Downs Syndrome, and in a remarkably frank conversation, Georgie once said: 'I remember the day Ollie was born and how Damon coped, and I never loved him more than I did then.' The Hill family are very close and down to earth, and Damon and Georgie take their responsibilities as parents very seriously. In their unpublicized roles as patrons of the Downs Association they have given hope and encouragement to countless other parents coping in a similar situation.

It was Georgie who provided a telling insight into Damon's motivations with a story she told when he graduated to racing in F1. 'When Frank finally signed Damon I was so relieved and happy. It was brilliant,

fantastic! It had been such a long wait. I wanted to run around, buy people flowers, have parties. I got annoyed with him. He was happy, of course, but then he just said matter-of-factly, "Okay, that's dealt with that. Let's get on to the next thing."'

When he lined up on the starting grid at Kyalami for the 1993 South African Grand Prix, Damon Hill was already regarded by the motorsport world as a racer in his own right, albeit one who was facing a make-or-break challenge. He was Graham Hill's son, but the scale of his own motor-racing achievements had already moved him clear of the shadow of his father's two World Championships long before he had led, let alone won, his first Grand Prix.

**F3000 (here, at Brands Hatch in 1990) was less kind as unreliability dogged the fledgling racer's efforts, but at least Hill proved that he had the speed required to lead races.**

# CHAPTER 3

In retrospect, much of Hill's early F1 career had all the hallmarks of a fairy tale. Plucked from the obscurity of an uncompetitive seat in the soon-to-succumb Brabham team, he landed the best ride in the sport when Frank Williams decided to give him the chance to race alongside Alain Prost in the 1993 season, 1992 World Champion Nigel Mansell having quit the team in high dudgeon and headed for America. Hill had already been the team's test driver for two years, but graduating to race status was a huge step and a golden opportunity that at a stroke made him the envy – and in some cases the enemy – of many struggling F1 aspirants.

From failing to qualify on occasions with Brabham, he now had the means to race with Prost and the Frenchman's legendary rival, Ayrton Senna, two of the greatest names in the sport and two of the undisputed stars of their era. And he did not disappoint. In that astonishing year he won three Grands Prix and, with only a little more luck, might have gone on to challenge Prost for the World Championship.

# LESSONS FROM THE PROFESSOR

Having landed F1's plum drive, Hill was under no illusions that the real challenge was just beginning, for Formula One is a business in which those who do not perform rarely stay for long. He knew this from his observation of events in the Brabham team in 1992. While he continued to test for Williams-Renault, and while Nigel Mansell that year continued to rack up victory after victory on his way to the world title, Hill waited his own turn to get behind the wheel on a Sunday afternoon.

He had tried out a turbocharged Benetton at Paul Ricard in 1988, courtesy of Peter Collins, the Williams, Benetton and Lotus team manager who had helped Mansell on his way. And in 1990 he had been invited to test interim Brabham chassis fitted with Yamaha engines, which the Chessington-based team would switch to in 1991. On both occasions the offers led to nothing further. The Benetton test was simply for experience, while his

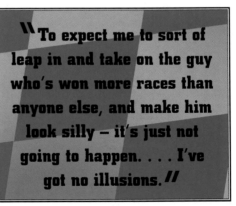

> **"To expect me to sort of leap in and take on the guy who's won more races than anyone else, and make him look silly – it's just not going to happen. . . . I've got no illusions."**

Middlebridge racing commitments in F3000 prevented him from accepting the Brabham offer and thus gaining more mileage. But he stuck close to Brabham, waiting, knowing it represented his best realistic chance of actually racing rather than simply testing. For while Frank Williams knew Hill could lead F3000 races, and that he could set fast lap times during test sessions, he was not about to take the risk of putting a rookie driver into the F1 racing team. Hill needed another means of demonstrating that side of his ability.

It finally came when Brabham's manager, Dennis Nursey, tired of Giovanna Amati's unsuccessful efforts to qualify the now Judd-powered BT60Bs, and also of waiting for her promised sponsorship to arrive. When the Spanish GP came around in May, Amati was out and the colours of the London Rowing Club adorned the helmet of the man who had replaced her. Initially his own efforts to make the grid were no more successful than the Italian's, though his lap times were much quicker. But in Britain he

succeeded in scraping on to the grid in 26th, and last, place. And he finished. As the crowd went berserk at Mansell's final British GP victory, and Mansell actually ran over one track invader, Hill brought his Brabham home in 16th place. Later, Hungary brought him another chance, and as Mansell clinched his championship, Hill finished 11th in the completely uncompetitive car.

Brabham folded before the end of the season, but Hill knew that the French Ligier team was interested in his services. He travelled to Adelaide for the

**At Silverstone in 1992 Hill brought the newly liveried Brabham BT60B home in 16th place amid the Mansellmania. The paint job helped make the cars look the part, thanks to team manager John MacDonald.**

> **" He would simply go away with the data and go through it with the engineers. . . . The next day he'd be right on the pace. That certainly impressed us. "**

last race simply to keep his face about in Formula One circles, where he was rapidly making many friends with the quiet and courteous profile that some found welcome distraction from Mansell's occasional histrionics. At the same time, Mansell's decision to defect to IndyCars in America, having failed to reach financial agreement with Williams, meant that a seat in the race team was also vacant for 1993. Alain Prost would be driving one car, which was part of the reason why Mansell was distressed, while the faithful Italian Riccardo Patrese had decided to spend his last season of F1 as Michael Schumacher's partner at Benetton, a decision he would surely regret.

The choice facing Frank Williams boiled down to Hill or fellow Briton Martin Brundle after Peter Collins had indicated his reluctance to part with either Johnny Herbert or Mika Hakkinen by placing vast transfer fees on their talented heads. If anything, the odds seemed to favour Brundle, with his vast F1 experience, but Hill knew Williams and Williams knew Hill. The winter months would be trying, particularly since Ligier couldn't be expected to hang on indefinitely waiting for Hill to make up his mind.

The prospect of occupying the second Williams-Renault seat alongside Prost was every racer's dream, even Senna's, and it was so tantalizingly close that

Hill could think of nothing else. It was there, just beyond his reach, and there was nothing he could do to influence the decision.

'The worst part', Hill recalled of that hiatus, 'was the thought that I might end up with nothing. I was warm about the Ligier chance, but on the one hand, with no disrespect to Ligier, I had the chance of the best drive in Formula One, and on the other the chance of a good drive in Formula One. I thought, "If I hang on for the best drive and the Ligier drive, Ligier can't wait much longer", and I stood a chance of losing both. And I thought, "Well, what do you do?" If I'd plumped for second best, how would I feel if Frank turned round and said, "Why didn't you wait? I would have given you a try with Williams if you'd just waited." I dared not try and put any pressure on him at the time.'

And Frank wasn't about to give any helpful hints. He actually gave Brundle to believe that he had got the drive, only to change his mind just as the older Briton thought he would be signing a contract. It was thus Brundle who went to Ligier, highly disillusioned and not a little disappointed, and Hill who was finally put out of his misery. On such whims do F1 fortunes turn.

No sooner had the official announcement been made than Hill asked the Fleet Street media not to expect too much of him too soon: 'I don't want to make any wild claims at all, it's unrealistic,' he said. 'To expect me to sort of leap in and take on the guy who's won more races than anyone else, and make

him look silly – it's just not going to happen. It's far more difficult, Formula One, than that. And I've got no illusions.'

Indeed he hadn't. He was well aware that not since Jackie Stewart had stepped into a BRM back in 1965 had a British driver graduated to F1 with such good equipment so early in his career. And since then only the Swiss Clay Regazzoni and the ill-fated Italian Ignazio Giunti had had similar fortune when they joined Jacky Ickx at Ferrari in 1970. Hill was conscious of the magnitude of the opportunity presented to him, and also of the pressures and jealousies it would evoke.

**Although the Brabhams were hopelessly uncompetitive, driving them gave Hill experience of tracks that would subsequently stand him in very good stead.**

**New beginning: Hill seems suitably uptight in this 1993 shot during his early racing apprenticeship with Williams.**

Williams's faith in signing Hill, who had just those two Grands Prix behind him, surprised some observers, particularly since it meant turning down Brundle, who had a reputation as a mediocre qualifier but a very strong racer. It was not something done lightly, either, which perhaps made comprehension of the decision all the harder for the latter.

South Africa was a disaster for Hill, who qualified fourth but spun out of second place on the opening lap and later collided with the Italian Alessandro Zanardi, but he quickly made amends with second places to Senna on the great Brazilian's home ground at Interlagos and in his own backyard at Donington. Each time he raced strongly and

performed more impressively than Prost, who spun in Brazil and spent much time switching back and forth from dry to wet tyres in a British race remarkable for Senna's brilliance and the changeable weather. Hill spun off the road in Imola, failed to finish in Spain after starting from the front row, but then finished second yet again to Senna in Monaco after Prost was unfairly penalized for an alleged jump start, and third in Canada.

By any standard he produced some highly impressive performances, but more were to come. At this stage of his F1 career Hill was learning fast, and while his driving drew much praise there were also disgruntled parties prepared to explain it by suggesting that the Williams was such a superior car that anybody with an ounce of talent could drive it. It would not be the last time that Hill would hear such suggestions, for they would dog him all along the road to the championship.

It was in France that he really began to show his potential, for there he took his first pole position in direct competition with Prost, who was determined to show well on his own, and Renault Sport's, home turf. In the race Prost came home the victor yet again, but Hill was literally only three tenths of a second behind – mere inches on the race track – having pushed him all the way. And there were very strong suggestions, denied weakly by Williams, that team orders had prevented the pair of them fighting it out. It was the first Grand Prix that Hill genuinely could have won.

Two more followed quickly. At Silverstone, where he was desperate to exorcise the ghost of his father's continued misfortune when attempting to win at home, he lost pole position to Prost but was leading the race from the Frenchman when he suffered a rare Renault engine failure. 'That', he admitted, 'was one of the most bitter defeats of my career.' But he drowned his sorrows with a quick pint of Labatt's – Williams's sponsor's brand – at the British Racing Drivers' Club as he walked back to the same hero's welcome that his father had received after spinning away the lead of the 1960 race. In Germany Prost was given an unwarranted 10 second stop-and-go penalty, which left Hill comfortably in the lead until a tyre punctured on his penultimate lap.

Prost won both of those races, but the tide of fortune would at last turn in Hill's favour in Hungary. Prost took pole position again, but Hill was left alone on the front row when the Frenchman's engine stalled, obliging him to start from the back. And though Prost set fastest lap while recovering, it was Hill who sped first beneath the chequered flag, etching the family name on a winner's trophy for the first time since Monaco in 1969, his father's last triumph. A fortnight later he repeated the feat at Spa in the Belgian GP, where Schumacher, Prost and Senna chased him home, and when Prost's engine broke at Monza, Hill completed a remarkable hat-trick.

Pole position in Portugal was negated when Hill's engine refused to fire on the warm-up lap and, like

Prost in Hungary, he had to start from the back. There he recovered to finish third, while Japan brought a less impressive fourth in the race in which Senna and newcomer Eddie Irvine had an on-track skirmish that later prompted the Brazilian to throw a punch at the Ulsterman. Hill rounded out the most impressive debut season in recent memory with third place in Australia behind Senna, who would shortly become his team leader at Williams, and Prost, who was heading for retirement. And he finished third behind them in the World Championship. He had succeeded beyond even his own wildest dreams, though there were still detractors banging the old drum of best car, best engine. As former World Champion Mario Andretti stressed, getting into the

**Team boss Frank Williams (right) and Williams' new signing Damon Hill eye each other warily at a press conference in autumn 1993. Williams was then and remains a man with very high expectations of his employees.**

best car is every driver's aim, and half the battle in mounting a serious title bid. In racing you make your own luck, and Hill's was running with him.

It falls to Patrick Head, as it frequently does, to provide sensible perspective on the situation, bringing to it his rational, engineer's way of thinking. 'It's easy for people to pigeon-hole Damon,' he said. 'But he had not stabilized fully by then. He was still absorbing information and learning from it. Quite possibly he did have a better engine and car in 1993, but by the end of that year he had still won one more Grand Prix than Michael Schumacher and he could have won twice that number. I think Damon's performance was pretty remarkable for a guy in his first year.'

Without question, Hill had benefited from racing in an era in which technology monitored a driver's every move in the cockpit, and from a team in which the leader's telemetry was available for assessment by a junior driver. It certainly helped him that he could overlay the telemetry from Prost's car on his own, so that he could make immediate assessment of the places where he was gaining and those where he was losing out. And by doing so, rectify his shortcomings. If he was slow, he was able to sort it out by this meticulous analysis of Prost's figures. It mattered not at all that others might not have been able to do so in bygone eras; this was the modern day, and that was simply the way that the game was played. It was not Damon Hill's fault that times had changed; he simply

**From the ridiculous to the sublime. When Hill finally graduated to the Williams race team as Alain Prost's partner in 1993, it was a far cry from the struggle with the Brabhams the previous season.**

made full use of the weapons in the armoury afforded by the new technologies available, as others had made use of the first monocoque chassis or the first aerofoils.

Head made other telling points, too. 'Damon has a fierce determination. I didn't know his father well, but Graham was that way and Damon is too. Determination is obviously a characteristic that has been handed over in the genes.

'His performance didn't really surprise us much because we knew what he could do after all the testing he'd done for us. But I admired his resourcefulness. At times he would come up against a brick wall of a lap time one day, and he'd be wringing his hands about it, but he appreciated the technical nature of the problem and he would simply go away with the data and go through it with the engineers. He would compare it with Alain's, and then he'd get it all worked out. The next day he'd be right on the pace. That certainly impressed us.'

It also impressed Williams that Hill would go his own way in setting up his car, showing an independence and maturity that were unusual in a rookie. He would only take over Prost's settings if the situation had become so desperate that there really was no other option. That is another mark of a top driver.

'There were several times', Head continued, 'where you could say very markedly that Damon took a major step forward overnight. I'm not sure whether he'd get back to his hotel room and do mantras or chanting or whatever, but I suspect he simply sat

down and studied everything in minute detail until he'd worked out exactly where he was losing time, and then figured out what he had to do about it.'

All of this was just as well, because in 1994 he would be paired with the most formidable team-mate of them all, Ayrton Senna, whose own speed and ability to sift through and assimilate technical data was already part of motorsport lore.

**Racing drivers rely heavily on the support of their back-up team, especially their race engineer. Here Williams' technical director, Patrick Head, encourages his driver.**

# CHAPTER 4

The tragedy of Ayrton Senna's death early in the 1994 season ripped the Williams-Renault team apart and sent shock waves through a sport whose competitors had brutally been brought face-to-face with their own mortality. The Brazilian former champion had been expected to dominate the year as he joined Hill to lead Williams, but upon his demise the responsibility of leading the team and maintaining its World Championship challenge fell squarely on Hill's shoulders, just as his father had had to lead Lotus back from the darkness in 1968 when Jim Clark was killed. And to add to the burden, Hill had to do it just as Michael Schumacher was emerging as Senna's heir apparent and the world was coming to appreciate the young German's astonishing talent.

In a bloody year characterized by acrimony, controversy and accusations of cheating levelled against a top team, Hill pushed Schumacher and Benetton to the limit, and the great confrontation at the final race in Adelaide when Schumacher pushed Hill off the track and thus won his first World Championship, proved a fitting epitaph to a season in which the sporting rulebook had yet again been rewritten.

# SHOULDERING THE BURDEN

Formula One fans across the globe awaited the 1994 season in full anticipation that it would set the stage for further domination by Ayrton Senna, now that he had once again manoeuvred himself back into what was unquestionably the best car in the game for the first time since 1988. Instead, it was to be a year in which so many circumstances for Damon Hill echoed the tragedy that his father Graham had had to face when Jim Clark died in 1968, and in which the loss of Senna would sweep him into the limelight on a riptide of the uncertainty that some felt about his ability to rise to the occasion, and the expectation of others that he would do just that.

Hill and Senna had already encountered one another wheel-to-wheel on the race track throughout 1993, and in that year's San Marino Grand Prix at Imola Damon had laid down a marker. After a heady three-way fight between Hill, Prost and Senna was eventually resolved in Prost's favour ahead of Senna, and Hill had slid off the road into retirement, he was summoned by the Brazilian to be ticked off for getting in the way. Hill, still a relative newcomer to F1, was polite but unmoved by the outburst. 'I simply told him that I didn't think I had done anything that I hadn't seen him do to other people on many occasions,' he said, straight-faced.

Now that Senna was his teammate, many expected Hill to be annihilated by the triple World Champion. The detractors who were envious of the chance that Frank Williams had given him in 1993 sat back and waited for him to be put in his place. And in qualifying for the first two races he was. Senna was fastest in each, a long way ahead of his partner. But Senna retired each time, whereas Hill came through to finish second in Brazil. Of course, it will never be known whether he would ever have challenged Senna, and the sceptics scoff at the very suggestion even today. But at the end of 1993 Williams' chief designer

> **"I simply told him that I didn't think I had done anything that I hadn't seen him do to other people on many occasions."**
> **Hill on Senna after a wheel-to-wheel on the track**

**Opposite: This is what the modern racing driver has to 'endure' at least twice a day during a Grand Prix weekend. Hill, hidden among the world's motorsport journalists, tells them how it was out there.**

Adrian Newey had offered an interesting insight into Hill's modus operandi and how he might deal with a man who had a reputation for destroying team-mates, even those of the calibre of Prost, and unsettling them to the point where they were so out-psyched that they could not even drive to their usual level of ability.

'I don't think that will be the case because Damon is very gritty,' said Newey thoughtfully, adding by way of further explanation: 'The first time that he and Alain [Prost]did a race distance together was during testing at Estoril, and Alain was blindingly quick. It was his first race distance for us, whereas Damon had done several but finished way behind him. But by the end of the year Damon was right there. He'd worked it out, thought about it, and adjusted his driving style where he needed to. That's his great asset.'

Hill was the archetypal driver of the modern era, a technocrat who could read telemetry and use it to analyze and overcome any shortcomings. It didn't matter that some others might see that as an unfair advantage. That was how racing was, and he took full advantage of it. It had always been the name of the game. And he professed to have no fears about his new partner's supposed ability to crush him mentally. 'What's he going to do?' he demanded to know at an early season press conference. 'Put me in a Vulcan Mind grip?'

It was not the brash comment that it sounds, for it was made with Hill's usual disarming smile. He had been measured, after all, against high-calibre drivers right from the first moment he sat in a Williams, and having Nigel Mansell and then Alain Prost as

**With Alain Prost's retirement, prompted when he learned that, regardless of Prost's feelings on the matter, Frank Williams had hired Ayrton Senna for 1994, Hill's Williams FW16 bore the number zero. Number one is traditionally reserved for the reigning World Champion, and thus hasn't been seen on a Williams for a good few years.**

team-mates was no sinecure for an inexperienced driver whom many expected to stumble. 'When you are used to having such people as your team-mates,' he said more seriously, 'you just accept the situation. And why worry? You get into F1 wanting to be the best, and very few drivers get the chance to be measured against the best at such an early stage. I would far rather be a man who had won against such strong team-mates rather than skirt the issue all the time.'

In both of those opening races, at Interlagos in Brazil and then Aida in Japan, Senna had sensationally been beaten by an unexpected rival – Michael Schumacher in the Benetton-Ford. The German had already impressed everyone since making a startling debut for Jordan in 1991, but even he had not been expected to challenge the great Senna quite so soon. But nobody could know as they lined up for the third round of the 1994 World Championship, the San Marino Grand Prix, that the 'old order' of Formula One was about to be changed, brutally and forever.

Imola is a circuit that everyone loves, for the Italian fans endow it with a unique atmosphere of enthusiasm and history. But the 1994 meeting had a macabre quality that manifested itself on Friday when Senna's young protégé Rubens Barrichello was extremely fortunate to escape with nothing worse than a broken nose after crashing his Jordan-Hart at very high speed. Then the young Austrian driver Roland Ratzenberger became the first man in eight years to die in an F1 car when he crashed his Simtek during qualifying on Saturday afternoon. Both

incidents upset Senna profoundly, for he had a deep-seated concern for the welfare of fellow drivers that was not always evident when he was racing them wheel-to-wheel. At one time he had talked of not starting. Yet he knew that Imola offered him his best chance of beating Schumacher and getting his Championship challenge underway, and as the underdog he knew he could not afford to fritter away such opportunities.

The air was charged with tension as Senna led the field away from pole position, and it was heightened further as, behind the leaders, another accident occurred on the startline. Senna continued to lead

**By the time that Senna stepped aboard at Williams (left), Hill was well used to high-powered team-mates, having worked with Mansell and raced alongside Prost. Their relationship was not particularly warm but it never really had much chance to get off the ground.**

In 1968 Graham Hill carried the burden as a shattered Lotus team tried to come to terms with the death of Jim Clark. When Ayrton Senna died at Imola in 1994 Damon found himself fulfilling much the same role. On that fateful day he drove to a delayed sixth place. He was at that point unaware precisely what had caused his illustrious team-mate to crash, and his performance that afternoon ranks among the bravest in F1's rich history. Once free of the great Brazilian's shadow, Hill would continue his winning ways, here at the British GP.

Schumacher at reduced speed as the debris was cleared away while they circulated behind a safety car, and the racing resumed on the sixth lap. One lap later Senna's Williams-Renault failed to negotiate the flat-out left-hand corner called Tamburello which followed the start/finish line. The telemetry would later reveal that he managed to scrub off 60mph by braking very hard before the car smashed into the unyielding concrete wall on the outside of the bend at 130mph, but the right front wheel flailed back into the cockpit on the sinews of its broken suspension arms, and inflicted fatal injuries.

When the race was restarted Schumacher won yet again as Hill trailed home sixth after a brush with the German early on. Few of F1's stunned retinue had any stomach for further competition, but this was a particularly brave drive since nobody at that stage could say with any accuracy what had caused Senna's accident. Even today it continues to be a matter for conjecture.

Hill was no stranger to death in his chosen profession, though mercifully it now occurred much less frequently than it had in his father's heyday. Back in 1986 his plans to race F3 with Dick Bennetts' crack West Surrey Racing team had foundered when Bennetts' lead driver Bertrand Fabi was killed during pre-season testing at the Goodwood circuit in West Sussex, prompting Bennetts to change his plans.

That incident inevitably made Hill question his enthusiasm for the sport, but he had already seen such moments. 'The darker side of it is thankfully rare, but I remember Dad coming home one day very,

very quiet and saw the news film of Jim Clark's death, though I wasn't too sure what it all meant. I was only eight.' Now he was the one returning home to his own children, shouldering the awful burden of knowledge that Clark's spiritual successor, Ayrton Senna, had followed the Scot into history.

'When Bert was killed I took the conscious decision that I wasn't going to stop,' he said. 'It's not just competing, it's doing something exciting. I'm at my fullest skiing, racing or whatever. And I'm more frightened of letting it all slip and reaching 60 and finding I've done nothing. I was in for a penny, and I'd be in for the £100,000. I decided I'd still go for it, but the most crucial of all, I'd do it to the fullest, not half-heartedly.' It could have been his father speaking. Like any other couple in F1, Hill and his wife Georgie talked things over in great depth after Imola, and decided to go forward. After Mika Hakkinen had taken him out of the Monaco Grand Prix, which Schumacher won, Hill triumphed in Spain when the German's car stuck in fifth gear. Again it was history repeating itself, for Graham Hill had helped to revive the shattered Lotus team with victory in the Spanish GP.

Initially, David Coulthard was drafted in as Hill's partner when the German driver Heinz-Harald Frentzen turned down an offer from Williams and elected to stay with Sauber. But behind the scenes Renault Sport chief Patrick Faure shored up his reservations about Hill's ability to get the job done by falling back on an old stager. For a staggering

£6,000,000 Nigel Mansell was dragged back from IndyCar racing, ostensibly to lead the Williams campaign. He would compete in France, which did not clash with his existing commitments, and then do the three final races.

Hill drew no small measure of satisfaction when he outqualified and outraced Mansell at Magny-Cours, but both were beaten again by Schumacher. And then came the British GP at Silverstone, where Schumacher was penalized (and later excluded from two races) for overtaking Hill illegally on the grid formation lap and then ignoring the black flag which informed him of the infringement. The governing

**In 1994 Hill was reunited with Nigel Mansell, the exiled World Champion, whose seat he had taken at Williams for the 1993 season.**

body, the FIA, was accused of trying to repay Schumacher and the Benetton team for alleged technical infringements, evidence of which its boffins had been unable to find. But whatever the political machinations in an increasingly uneasy season, it would provide a golden opportunity for Hill and Williams to claw back some of their lost advantage. Schumacher beat Hill in Hungary, but was then disqualified from his victory in Belgium, which went to Hill. FIA officials decreed that a plank of wood beneath Schumacher's car, designed to act as a skid plate, was not of the regulation depth.

Hill then won in Italy and Portugal in Schumacher's enforced absence, before the German returned to beat him convincingly in Spain at the Grand Prix of Europe. Hill's only consolation there was that he had again outdriven the returning Mansell.

The 1994 World Championship thus moved forward to a showdown, first in Japan, then in Australia. If Schumacher won in the Far East it was all over; if Hill won at the Suzuka track, he could prolong his Championship hopes.

Whenever talk turns to that race, a light shines in Hill's dark eyes at the recollection of one of his all-

In three out of four races Hill out-qualified 'Il Leone', but Mansell took pole for the Australian GP. Following Hill's astonishing victory in Japan, the controversial 1994 World championship came down to a shoot-out between the Briton and Michael Schumacher in Adelaide, where they both got the jump on Mansell and set the scene for the acrimony that would follow.

time favourites. And his comments reveal the oft-concealed motivation that really drives this most reserved of racing drivers. Some drive simply to beat others, but Hill's first rival has always been himself, and he has constantly pushed himself to see just what he is capable of achieving. In Japan that day, the result was greatness.

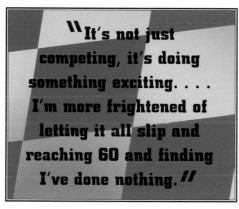

**"It's not just competing, it's doing something exciting. . . . I'm more frightened of letting it all slip and reaching 60 and finding I've done nothing. //**

on his back, had the necessity arisen.

'I like to keep in contact with the team during a race, via the radio,' he said. 'They'd tell me the gap to Michael at the beginning of each lap. So at the first corner I'd keep getting the message: "He's closing on you, he's closing on you!" And I would reply, "I know. I know!"'

'Suzuka was. . . Well, I don't think it was so much winning the race, as the fact that I drove on a completely different level. In what I would call a sort of twilight zone of driving. You were just offering yourself up, completely, to your instincts. It was fantastic. Just an awesome feeling. The satisfaction from having won that was tremendous.'

It was even greater because the race was held in appalling conditions, with torrential rain and extremely poor visibility. And to make matters worse, during his pit stop the team had only been able to change three of his four tyres because the left rear wheel refused to part company with its hub. Not surprisingly, the team kept this information from him at the time. Hill laughed. 'They didn't come on the radio and say: "Oh, by the way, your rear tyre is knackered." That would have made things worse, because they don't normally last the whole race, but I still had three good ones.' And on that, his day of days, he would have carried the Williams to first place

But Schumacher did not close enough in this gripping encounter, and Hill stayed ahead to win brilliantly. After a season of see-saw tension the two of them went to Adelaide for the last race with Schumacher only one point ahead and everything to play for.

This time Mansell upstaged them both in qualifying, taking pole position and forcing Schumacher into an error which saw him crash heavily trying to beat the lap time. But Mansell made mistakes on the opening lap, and Schumacher and Hill sped away into the battle that everyone had desperately hoped for. Lap after lap Hill dogged Schumacher's wheeltracks, pushing here, applying pressure there. He was driving superbly. But when they came up to lap Frentzen, Hill lost a little ground and was just under three seconds behind Schumacher when the German made an unprovoked error, lost control of his Benetton and slid into a concrete wall on the 36th lap. He recovered just as Hill arrived at the scene, and

**Opposite: Almost over —
and definitely out. In the
inset photograph Hill
tried to find sufficient
space to avoid a collision
as Schumacher chops
ruthlessly back onto the
racing line. The German
had just hit the wall
before the corner and
was trundling on the
left-hand side of the
track when Hill lined up
for the corner. The
Benetton was an instant
retirement, but when Hill
had to do likewise with
damaged suspension,
Schumacher's extra point
was enough to clinch him
a tainted World
Championship.**

momentarily appeared to pull to the left to let his rival through. Perhaps at that stage he was assessing possible damage before realizing he could still win the title; perhaps he received orders over the radio. Nobody would ever offer any enlightenment. Instead, as Hill dived for the inside line to grab the lead, Schumacher cut with ruthless precision back across the Williams and they made contact. The Benetton was pitched up on to its left-hand wheels before crashing back down and out of the race; Hill swept on. He needed to finish only second to win the crown, but his left front tyre was deflated. He struggled round to the pits, still in contention, but then the team discovered that the pushrod in the car's left front suspension was too

badly damaged to continue, and Hill too was out of the race.

Further round the track the news was relayed to a jubilant Schumacher, who punched the air with both hands. Back in the Williams pit, Hill's expression said it all. The tragic, acrimonious season was over, and he had lost. But he said nothing afterwards to condemn his rival's tactics, which many observers felt were completely unacceptable and would have been more in keeping on a dodgem track.

Damon Hill kept his emotions in check and took defeat with engaging dignity. He had been pushed out of the World Championship, but he had lost with honour.

# CHAPTER 5

Hill's 1995 campaign got off to a spectacular start in Brazil, where he led easily until his Williams broke down, handing victory to Schumacher's Benetton. But when the Briton bounced back to win the next two races it seemed that he was finally on target for the elusive Championship crown. Williams had the best car, and Schumacher was struggling.

But, as in the previous two seasons, hope proved to be a chimera. Schumacher and Benetton piled on the pressure with relentless force as the German headed towards a second consecutive World Championship, and this time there was no controversy to provide distraction from their superiority.

Instead of crowning him, 1995 degenerated into a season in which Hill's predominantly private and reserved character would be probed mercilessly by the world's media, and his every move or statement became front-page news. His formerly supportive countrymen in Fleet Street alternately praised him to the skies and then tore him apart as they vented their spleen upon his failure to live up to the expectations they had generated.

And though he could not know it at the time, it was the year in which the seeds of his Williams downfall in 1996 were to be sown.

# UP ON THE PEDESTAL

The year of 1995 should have been the one in which Damon Hill would claw his way to the top slot that Schumacher's ruthlessness had denied him the previous season. Instead, it proved to be another nightmare, a chimera that smiled upon him to begin with before turning on him viciously.

Those who had expected the near miss of 1994 to blunt Hill's competitive edge made the same mistake as those who had written off Nigel Mansell when in 1986, also in Australia, his championship aspirations had exploded along with his right rear tyre. Like Mansell, Hill showed a core of steely determination and bounced back in style. Schumacher was staying with Benetton for the new season, joined by Hill's old F3 nemesis Johnny Herbert, but though they too had Renault power now, it was Hill who dominated the opening race in Brazil. He was walking the race when his suspension failed on the 31st lap. Schumacher won, having initially been disqualified for an alleged fuel discrepancy. This was not good news, but the Williams had shown a clear advantage.

It would keep it for the next two races, the Argentinian and San Marino Grands Prix, where Hill won comfortably to increase his championship lead. Going in to the Spanish race in May he had 20 points to Schumacher's 14, but there Hill's season showed the first signs of falling apart as Schumacher and Benetton pulled off a thoroughly convincing victory that was made even worse by the Williams-Renault faltering from second place within sight of the flag. Damon was lucky to roll home fourth, and when he was critical of his car's state of reliability, he was none too gently reminded afterwards by Frank Williams that Williams was a team that won together and lost together. It would mark the first outward manifestation of the friction that was building within the Didcot outfit.

Monaco brought a sublime pole position for Hill which should have laid to rest once and for all any doubts about his latent speed, for he eclipsed Schumacher by eight-tenths of a second in a

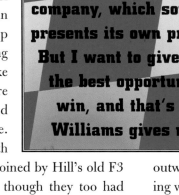

*"I've grown within the company, which sometimes presents its own problems. But I want to give myself the best opportunity to win, and that's what Williams gives me."*

**Opposite: Like Mansell, defeat only strengthened Hill's resolve. In the early races of the 1995 season, he and the Williams-Renault FW17 were the class of the field as Schumacher and Benetton struggled.**

nail-biting shoot-out in the closing minutes of qualifying around the barrier-lined street circuit. Race day, however, provided another shattering blow to Hill's morale. What had been a superbly balanced car in qualifying now behaved badly. Track conditions had changed and he found the Williams plagued with serious understeer, just the problem a driver doesn't want on a circuit where a car's ability to turn into the tight corners is a key part of quick lap times. Schumacher romped away to win by a crushing 33.5 seconds, leaving Hill and Williams to pick over the bones of a technical argument about the benefits of the differential they had elected to run. Schumacher, having edged one point ahead in Spain, was now the series leader by five and the tide was running ominously in his favour.

Canada brought no relief. For once the Benetton ran into trouble, but Hill was in no position to benefit after yet again being blown away, for the Renault V10's hydraulic pump had failed once more, leaving him to coast to a halt by the pit wall. Worse was to follow.

Damon had pole position again in France, but by the end of the race Benetton's general superiority in fuel stops and teamwork in the pits had reversed the deficit; Hill finished second again to Schumacher, 31 seconds adrift in the race, 11 points behind in the championship.

By this stage of the year there were open murmurings that Williams had far and away the

best car, but that its drivers were failing to take full advantage of its superiority. This may or may not have been true. Certainly, the Williams seemed to handle better than the Benetton. Herbert found the pointy turn-in of the latter, and its inherent tail-happy oversteer, was incompatible with his driving style, whereas Schumacher, who called the shots, revelled in such a set-up and exploited its ability to stick tight to his chosen line entering a corner, while using his scintillating reflexes to sort out any sliding on the exit. Schumacher was on a roll, he had the team working solely for him, and was making every other driver look at best second rate.

Hill, on the other hand, was working for a team which places the emphasis purely on engineering and does nothing to cosset its drivers. And in David Coulthard, who by now was recovering from the debilitating effects of tonsillitis, he had a team-mate capable of upsetting the internal equilibrium – and, more crucially, fully permitted to by the team's management.

'I'm very happy here,' Hill affirmed, 'but to some degree, in the back of your mind, you do wonder what it would be like somewhere else at times. I've been here for five years, and there's no point in changing just for the sake of it. But there's the possibility of being regarded as part of the furniture. I've grown within the company, which sometimes presents its

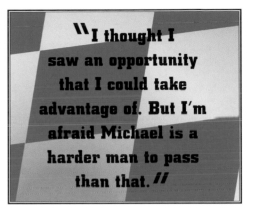

**"I thought I saw an opportunity that I could take advantage of. But I'm afraid Michael is a harder man to pass than that."**

**Opposite: The 1995 season started promisingly in Brazil for Hill, where only a suspension failure prevented him from burying the rest of the field.**

Schumacher pushes Hill in the early stages of the French Grand Prix at Magny-Cours in 1995. Better teamwork by Benetton saw the German home ahead of Hill.

own problems. But I want to give myself the best opportunity to win, and that's what Williams gives me.'

The British GP at Silverstone on 16 July marked the midpoint of the season, and Hill desperately wanted to win again on home ground. Once again he took pole position, and this time there were no silly incidents with Schumacher passing him on the warm-up lap. Instead, the World Champion got bogged down behind Jean Alesi's Ferrari, and Hill streaked away to build up a sizeable lead. When he made his first fuel stop Schumacher went ahead and opened a nine-second advantage, but nobody at Williams was unduly worried at this stage. Hill was catching up, and soon Schumacher would stop for fuel. Wouldn't he?

Hill already suspected the answer. One of the reasons why Alesi had been able to hold up the German was that Schumacher had elected to run a heavier fuel load initially. With awful realization, it began to dawn on Hill and Williams that the German, who was leading, was only going to stop once, whereas Damon, who should have been leading but wasn't, needed another stop. Schumacher stopped for just over 13 seconds on the 31st lap, just beyond half distance. Hill, spurred on by the crowd, began setting fastest laps as he edged his new lead out to 27 seconds, but it was not quite going to be sufficient to allow him to make his second stop without Schumacher regaining the lead. The scene was set for the debacle that followed. Hill made that stop on lap 41 and just as he reached the pitlane exit,

Schumacher swept by into the lead again. The chase was on. It ended ignominiously five laps later. Sweeping through the very fast Bridge corner and down into the braking area for the tight left-hander called Priory that follows, Hill thought he saw a gap as Schumacher momentarily left his turn-in late. From a long way back he tried an outbraking manoeuvre that was doomed from the outset. As Schumacher came over on his line, the two of them collided and speared off into the gravel bed. It was a misjudgement of catastrophic proportions, and the tabloid media had a field day at Hill's expense the next day, while fêting Herbert's first F1 victory. And as if matters could not have been worse, Frank Williams was alleged to have made disparaging remarks at Hill's expense which received wide airing on the printed page.

'I thought I saw an opportunity that I could take advantage of,' Damon said. 'But I'm afraid Michael is a harder man to pass than that.' He described their clash as a 'racing accident', and that was precisely what it was. Schumacher, this time the wronged party, made himself few friends by the arrogant assertion that: 'It was more or less the same situation as in Adelaide last year, where he also tried to dive inside where there was no room.' That, assuredly, it was not, and Schumacher of course knew that, but in the psychological war, as in the World Championship points stakes, he was emerging as the clear leader. Both of them were given a stern reprimand by the stewards, which seemed a trifle unfair on Schumacher.

Damon regained a measure of pride by taking pole position in front of Schumacher's adoring German fans at Hockenheim, and by making a terrific start to lead the first lap by almost two seconds, a massive margin on this very fast circuit. But going into the first corner he spun wildly out of control and had to endure catcalls as he trudged unhappily back to the pits. It seemed he had made yet another very embarrassing faux pas of monumental proportions, and much ink was devoted to questioning where the assurance he had displayed while winning the early season races had gone. Later, there were strong

**Hill regained the initiative over Schumacher with a masterful performance in the Hungarian GP, a victory described by the Englishman as 'the best race of my life'.**

masterful fashion after steadfastly repelling the Benetton driver's closest attentions, hope began to spring again. Hill had been dominant in qualifying, and Williams seemed to have recovered its momentum at last. 'It was', Damon said, 'the best race of my life.'

At Spa, however, Schumacher drove brilliantly on slick tyres on a track that had suddenly been dampened by rain but which almost as quickly began to dry out. It seemed that Hill had switched to rain tyres just at the right moment, but as he tried to overtake Schumacher the German was at his most ruthless, and after blocking him remorselessly began to draw away again as conditions improved. He won by 20 seconds, and his points lead grew to 15. Later, at the airport, Hill was asked why, during a bit of verbal fencing between himself and Schumacher at the post-race press conference, he had not been tempted to lose his temper when Schumacher was sanctimonious about tactics which even his most ardent admirers had felt to be excessively robust. Hill merely shrugged, and said: 'This is supposed to be a sport, isn't it? It seems that Michael is happy to use any means of preventing anybody else winning. I'm just not prepared to resort to similar tactics.'

The rest of the season was downhill all the way. At Monza there was further embarrassment when he inadvertently took Schumacher off again, misjudging his braking in a chicane while they were lapping the wandering Japanese backmarker Taki Inoue. 'It was just ridiculous,' Hill snapped. 'The guy just changed

**The difference between Hill and Schumacher was exemplifed during the race at Spa in 1995. The German's ruthlessness won him the day. Hill said: "I don't think motor racing should be a boxing match, but I suppose that's what people want these days."**

suggestions from Williams that a driveshaft bearing had begun to seize, precipitating Hill's demise.

'I think I have been around that corner enough times this weekend to know whether I am within the limit or not,' Hill said. But the damage had already been done. After his alleged criticism at Silverstone, there was a degree of suspicion that Frank Williams was belatedly bolting the stable door after letting another horse escape.

Schumacher now had an advantage of 19 points, but when he retired in Hungary and Hill won in

There were many
occasions during the
1995 season when Hill's
exit from the cockpit
came in a gravel bed.

lines twice in front of me. He let Schumacher past and then he blocked me and then moved out of the way again. Obviously Michael is very upset, but I'm upset too. I wanted a good race, and I would never ever want to tangle deliberately or have an accident like that.' He was extremely angry, but predictably he held it back with the remarkable restraint he had shown in Adelaide.

> "*The guy just changed lines twice in front of me. He let Schumacher past and then he blocked me and then moved out of the way again.*"

In Portugal Coulthard won his first Grand Prix, but Schumacher outfoxed Hill for second place. At the Nurburgring in Germany, for the Grand Prix of Europe, Hill got the better of Schumacher in some dramatic side-by-side racing, made a minor error which let his rival by again, and later clashed needlessly with Jean Alesi before crashing on his own and cracking a bone in his leg. In the back-to-back races in Japan, at Aida and then Suzuka, Schumacher ran rings round the Williams duo, and in the latter Hill suffered the humiliation of crashing out yet again. Schumacher had clinched the title in Aida, and in Suzuka merely rubbed salt into Williams' open wound as he equalled Mansell's record for nine wins in a single season. The atmosphere in the Williams team's small office at the circuit was thick enough to choke on. Hill's long-time supporter Patrick Head was barely able to speak civilly with his driver, and there was talk of acrimonious exchanges between

them on the car-to-pit radio during qualifying and the race.

In Australia meanwhile, as Adelaide prepared to host its last Grand Prix and to close out the 1995 season, 1980 World Champion Alan Jones, the man who won Williams its first title and by whom Frank and Patrick seemed to place such store, was busy cramming laconic criticism into a verbal shotgun before giving Hill both barrels at close range. Among other things, he accused him of procrastinating during races.

Hill took himself off for a quiet holiday between the two final races, to take stock of his shattered situation. He had seen the structure of hope and status that he had assiduously been building since 1993 shudder and collapse beneath him through a combination of Michael Schumacher's shockwave speed and confidence, and his own mistakes and misfortune. In 1995, when he was expected to win the World Championship, the new British Hero – who seemed to have the German's measure at the end of the traumatic 1994 season – had wobbled and fallen headlong into a nightmare of tabloid newspaper character assassination and recrimination within Williams.

If he were so inclined, Damon Hill might have told the tabloids where to go, and might have been moved to remind Jones that when the Australian drove for

*Opposite: Hill leads the fast-starting Alesi as Schumacher smokes at the beginning of the British GP at Silverstone in 1995. Hill looked set for victory.*

# CHAPTER 6

When Hill strode back into Adelaide for the last Grand Prix of the 1995 season, and stamped his authority on the race, he refused to acknowledge it as the rebirth that Fleet Street portrayed. He admitted, instead, that a holiday in Bali's Four Seasons Hotel with his wife Georgie had given him the time to refocus and to analyse and redefine his motivations and aspirations. It was, he said, the first time for many years that they had been away together without one or all of their three children. The previous race, the Japanese Grand Prix at Suzuka, had been so awful and his morale was so low that he hadn't known whether to laugh or cry.

In Australia Hill's performance once again threw his critics on to the back foot. They struggled to make sense of the remarkable turnaround and tried to find a fresh pigeon-hole into which to cram a man whose inconsistency on the track was rapidly rendering him one of the most enigmatic figures in motorsport.

# A FRESH FOCUS

Opposite: Dark, brooding
eyes and bushy brows;
the Hill trademarks. But
could a leopard change
its spots? Hill was
adamant he had learned
much from the drubbings
of 1995; Michael
Schumacher remained
sceptical.

Overleaf: Adelaide, 1995,
gave Hill one of the most
satisfactory victories of
his career. After the
disasters of Aida and
Suzuka, his holiday in
Bali left him rejuvenated
and clear-headed.
Brimful of confidence, he
was simply uncatchable.

The bare facts were these: Damon Hill took pole position for the Australian GP in Adelaide, blew Michael Schumacher into the weeds to record the 13th win of his career, and set fastest lap just in case anybody doubted his superiority. But even before he arrived Down Under he had also exorcised many of the demons that had bedevilled his unhappy year.

Hill is a victim of his benign nature. Whereas Mansell would exact revenge by freezing out critics or attempting to embarrass them in front of their peers, he lets the situation ride. 'I wouldn't say I'm easygoing,' he will admit, 'but I like to have a good relationship. I don't like confrontation. Maybe I should shun some people, but that's not part of my character. Maybe it should be.'

Several times in 1995 force of circumstance, allied to the inevitable pressures in modern 'sport', had dragged him into negative situations, but by Adelaide he had learned how to cope. It might have been late in the day, but it would set in train

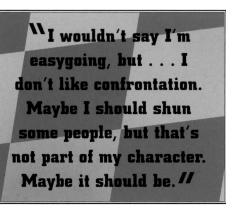

"I wouldn't say I'm easygoing, but . . . I don't like confrontation. Maybe I should shun some people, but that's not part of my character. Maybe it should be."

his ultimate championship success. 'My lesson from 1995 was that I got drawn into trying to recover from the lost momentum which we suffered in the early part of the season through mechanical problems. Instead of perhaps biding my time and staying in the fight, I went for the victory at all costs. And it was very costly! That's something which is not really my philosophy, so not being true to yourself and not sticking to what you know to be the right way of doing things was a bit of an error.' Being true to yourself is a key idea for Hill, indicating a character in which self-esteem surpasses other emotions. 'The times I have performed best are the times when I have done things my way,' he added, and a laugh deliberately robbed the statement of arrogance.

Damon Hill is a throwback to men such as Raymond Sommer, the great French privateer to whom the style in which the battle was fought was at least as important as the result. 'It's not as satisfying to win by default,' he insisted. 'It's got to be honourable. See, what sport should be about, and is about for me, is proving things to myself. I start with

the premise of "I don't know what I'm capable of doing, and I'm going to enter into a competitive environment to see what I am capable of doing." And I've found out more about myself doing this sport than I would ever believe possible. Some of the things I do, I come away feeling so incredibly proud of myself. That element is very important to me.

'If I drove absolutely brilliantly and I finished third and got a lot of criticism for it, that wouldn't bother me because I would know myself that I'd brought my performance to a level I considered the best I could do. You can only do your best. You can improve, but at a given time you can only do your best. If I felt I hadn't done my best I would hate myself, would tend to listen to criticism too much, and then life would become very uncomfortable. There are times when I have not been happy with my performance and have come in for a lot of criticism, and it's knocked the stuffing out of me.' There are very few topline racing drivers with the inner confidence to make such an admission.

Hill spent 1995 trying to hone a harder edge against his better nature. 'It's the real world of Formula One,' he said. 'A lot of factors have come to bear that I hadn't encountered before.' After the Belgian GP at Spa, where Schumacher had blocked and weaved, Hill had asked the FIA to clarify the rules on overtaking. This it did in a wishy-washy manner which effectively said that any tactic was acceptable, a so-called ruling that many observers believe will have negative long-term repercussions. After that Hill drove with greater aggression. But there was evidence that his style and manner isn't really suited to cut and thrust. 'I'm not happy with it,' he admitted. 'I don't think it's the picture of sport performed at its highest level that Formula One should be. I have my own view about it, but that's just my opinion of it. The fact is that Formula One will be performed in a certain way and I'm going to have to get on with it as it is.'

He was brought up in the era when his father and Jim Clark could race one another wheel-to-wheel without it ever entering either head to put the other in a dangerous or compromising position. They were no less successful nor competitive than their modern counterparts, but these were pre-Senna days before on-track aggression became part of a driver's armoury. Days when the game was played to a different set of rules, which the gentlemanly Hill continues to value.

It became fashionable – and therefore tempting – to label Damon Hill as something of a humourless enigma. One minute he was the former champion's son who went from zero to hero, the next the hard-luck Brit shoved out of championship success by his ruthless arch-rival. Then he was the Great British Hope torn apart for mucking things up with a series of rash manoeuvres. By the beginning of 1996 he was pushing ahead again in the World Championship as if he'd never had a gut-wrenching setback in his entire career. Enigma, yes. Humourless? Only to those unfortunate enough not to have spent sufficient time with him to appreciate his wider perspective on life. The truth is less prosaic. Hill is not out to race to appease his fans or his critics, but to prove he can do it to himself. When he dragged himself up from the depths to leave behind the embarrassment of Suzuka last year, and to dominate in Adelaide, Frank Williams was moved to suggest he was a new man. But he was simply falling back on his instincts and letting his old self, his obstinate, stubborn, rational old self, call the shots.

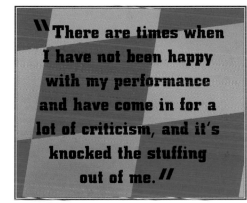

**" There are times when I have not been happy with my performance and have come in for a lot of criticism, and it's knocked the stuffing out of me. "**

'I know I can drive well and I just don't like it if I don't fulfil myself,' he reiterated in Argentina, early in the 1996 campaign. 'I knew I could do a better job in 1995, and fundamentally I just wanted to enjoy myself. I got to the point last year when I just didn't enjoy what I was doing and I couldn't possibly perform to my ultimate level.'

So he went away before Adelaide, and had a long look in a mirror, figuratively and, probably, literally. And he asked himself some fundamental questions.

'Yeah! Whether or not I wanted to do it! There are a number of reasons for doing Formula One, and if it were simply for the money that wouldn't be good enough reason. There's too much risk involved. And I came to the conclusion that that certainly wasn't part of the reason for doing it.' Money, to most successful race drivers who have moved beyond the 'poverty' level of their less fortunate competitors, simply becomes a means of establishing one's worth in an insular society that is obsessed with the folding stuff.

Hill maintains that one question he did not have to ask himself was whether he was good enough to do it. 'I always knew I was good enough, but I wondered if it was right for me to be doing it. And I came to the conclusion that it was. I'd got something to give and I just needed to give myself the right environment in which that flourishes, in which that side of me could come out.'

He sounded slightly evasive when it was suggested that by Adelaide he had sunk as low as he possibly could and was then starting to bounce back. But in truth he was just picking his words carefully, as he is wont to. 'I just decided that I wanted to go back and enjoy it. I didn't want to give it up. The thought of going through an entire season like the last few races of last year' – he gave a rueful laugh born of the memory of all the tail-between-legs journeys home from disappointment – 'was just an unbearable thought! I needed to be enjoying what I was doing. I felt more relaxed and more comfortable and I still feel that way. I'm driving better and I'm enjoying myself.'

By Argentina many things had changed, and with

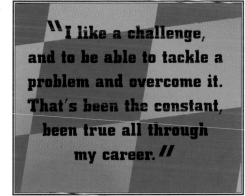

**" I like a challenge, and to be able to tackle a problem and overcome it. That's been the constant, been true all through my career. "**

Schumacher now at Ferrari he held the best hand in the poker game that is F1. And he was confident that he was well past the crisis point of 1995, and strong enough to deal with opposition better, as and when it might arise. 'I'm pretty confident that I'm not saying these things because I've had a run of success. I think, in actual fact, that it's the other way round. I've had a run of success because I feel better about what I'm doing. But I am prepared also for the downs. There are going to be downs this season, we'll have those weekends.'

**Opposite: Jacques Villeneuve desperately wanted to win on home ground in Canada, on the circuit named after his father. But Hill was again in dominant mood. Jacques would have to wait until Silverstone to get his own back.**

The fire of 1995 had tempered his edge, given it greater cutting power, and the manner in which he came through the test was a graphic indication of his basic character, and an echo of his father's riposte 'Beat that, you buggers' which followed a quick practice lap.

'I like a challenge, and to be able to tackle a problem and overcome it. That's been the constant, been true all through my career. I've not really come through in the conventional way, I suppose. You only have to look at how old I was when I started. I was 24 before I did my first full season in Formula Ford. The people I'm racing against these days are mostly 24! And they're already in Formula One.'

At this stage, admittedly when the opposition had been less than red hot, his relationship with Frank Williams and Patrick Head was a lot stronger, for all of them had gone through an introspective winter. But he reacted defensively when the matter was raised in conversation. 'Frank and Patrick have shown a lot of faith in me; right from the very start they've shown a lot of faith in me and given me the breaks.'

Yet things got very strained at times in 1995, and at Suzuka in particular the three of them were quite clearly not going to any ball games together.

'Well, nobody was happy with the way things were going,' he countered quickly. 'We were up there shooting for the title and we didn't win it. It was a big disappointment. Now we are prepared for anything this year. And whatever happens we are going to fight as a team. I think it's a characteristic not only of myself but also of the Williams team that they close ranks and move forward together. And a lot of that comes from the top, from Frank and Patrick.'

Those close to him say that by the start of 1996 he was enjoying taking on greater responsibility within the team, that he wanted a greater say over some of the things that might influence his future. 'I'm happy to take on more responsibility this year,' he confirmed, but lest the remark be misinterpreted he added qualification. 'I think I've always been allowed that responsibility, but I think that because I came up as a junior in the team, for a long time I assumed that the

**Photogenic, and often slightly wistful, Hill is an enigmatic figure to those who prefer their racing drivers to conduct their lives with a ruthless swagger. To those who believe in sport, fair play and reward for dedication, however, he is a champion worthy of respect.**

responsibility was theirs and that my responsibility was simply to drive the car. It's been a slow process of first of all trying to assume responsibility, and that responsibility being given to me slightly reluctantly.

'For instance, when Ayrton died I wanted to take on the responsibility. And I drove, I felt, to give the team back hope that they could win without him. But there were always those doubts, and I could understand that because it was only my second season.' That, of course, was when Renault Sport chief Patrick Faure still favoured Nigel Mansell in the middle of 1994.

Since then plenty of water, a lot of it perspiration from the Williams team, had flowed beneath the Bridge of Sighs. One World Championship was taken away by force, the other lost through a series of errors and misjudgements that were pretty evenly shared between Hill and Williams. It was early days in Argentina, and Flavio Briatore of Benetton was happy to remind anyone who would listen that there were still 13 races left as F1 people gathered for a beer at the airport, but things within the Didcot team already had a 'right' feeling about them.

Hill gave one of his dark smiles. 'I get the feeling that we've gone through a sort of fermentation process and now we are blended nicely.'

In 1995 Benetton's pit stop strategy consistently appeared to be superior to Williams', but those who witnessed Hill's race in Interlagos could not fail to have been impressed how well the calculated gamble paid off, even if Benetton's strategy was identical.

Damon savoured the memory of that breakthrough moment, with the clear confidence of a man who did not expect it to prove a one-off. 'That was perfect timing, and it was as much to do with the force of the pit stop – we couldn't go any further because we didn't have much fuel left to go any further. And it just happened to coincide with the right time on the track, I felt, to go to slicks. So when they said on the radio to come in for slicks, I just said: "That's absolutely fine by me, because it's the right time. Let's go for it." We got a lucky break and it didn't rain again. We've been to races where it's gone the other way simply because the weather changed unpredictably. But it went well.'

That weekend was altogether perfect as he annihilated the opposition in qualifying while cleverly harvesting tyres from his FIA-governed allocation of 28 per meeting, and when everything became a

**Hill met his opposition head-on at the French GP at Magny-Cours in July, where he scored his sixth win of the season. At that point the World Championship seemed a foregone conclusion.**

lottery just before the start with a downpour that could have spoiled everything, he came through the test. It was a satisfying weekend, but it took him no time to put it into perspective. 'It was a tricky race, but it wasn't one where I felt I had extended myself as much as I have in other races.'

His goal was simple as he bounced back, just as Nigel Mansell did after his near-misses in 1986 and '87. 'It's to perform better, and to try and win races.'

**To the victor, the spoils, and on the observers the spray of Moët et Chandon. In his four seasons with Williams-Renault Damon Hill became rather adept at uncorking the bubbly, thanks to a strike rate bettered only by Jim Clark and Juan Manuel Fangio.**

When it was suggested that 1995 had, in retrospect, been a crucible that had forged a stronger driver, the Hill humour surfaced as a dark grin and a knitting of those thick eyebrows. 'What, you mean like sort of being glazed? It is like steel being tempered, and you do feel like you've been hit with a hammer! I've certainly been hammered a few times!'

He knew that things would not be so clear-cut when the European season gathered pace as they had been in Australia and South America as the 1996 season unfolded, but his winter fitness programme with Schumacher's former trainer, Erwin Gollner, had already paid dividends in terms of physical and mental fitness. 'I worked harder and better over the winter,' Hill explained. 'I now have a gym at home, so I train more regularly. I even spent some time in Rio with Erwin so I could continue my training programme. I enjoy it, and I feel quite a lot sharper than I did last year.'

Every sportswriter has heard such things when boxers talk good fights, only to wither on the big night. Even as Hill voiced his thoughts, Frank Bruno had recently keeled over early when the chips were down with Mike Tyson. But Hill had revealed not a single crack in his new make-up while dominating the first three heavyweight rounds, and the variety and cohesiveness of his driving suggested he was more than ready to win his first championship.

The most appealing thing about him is his sense of sportsmanship, allied to the sense of humour that the media beyond racing like to think he lacks. He

Sadly, it was tears which flowed at Monaco rather than champagne. Here Hill leads the soon-to-depart Schumacher, Alesi, Berger, Barrichello and Irvine up the hill to Massenet in a race that he completely dominated until the rare engine failure that would later cause such anguish when the 10 lost points would have made all the difference in the battle with Villeneuve.

lapped Schumacher's Ferrari in Brazil, yet showed no signs of gloating afterwards no matter how satisfying it might have been inside. 'It was just one of those things,' he said matter-of-factly. 'I didn't even think about it. As I went past I just thought, "Oh." Not, "I'm lapping Michael Schumacher!" He didn't enjoy it; I probably enjoyed it much more than he did! But it's not the way I would have preferred to race him. It's much more fun racing him for the lead.'

It would transpire that he would have little need to race Schumacher for the lead in 1996. He had the speed and knew he could still win races as he faced the gruelling European season, but also he knew that he needed to maintain his freshly-honed consistency and forget the psychological wounds that he had shrugged off prior to Adelaide. Former triple World Champion Jackie Stewart publicly backed him to win the title, and so did Alan Jones. But Damon Hill himself knew that, good start notwithstanding, his fourth big year in Formula One would either make or break him. It was as simple and straightforward as that, and he would not have wanted it to be any other way.

# INDEX